BERNIE,

YOU'RE A BOOTLEGGER!

A Family's Escapades during the Prohibition Era

Joan Winghart Wilcox Sullivan

Order this book online at www.trafford.com
or email orders@trafford.com

Most Trafford titles are also available at major online book retailers.

Printed in the United States of America.

ISBN: 978-1-4269-3453-7 (sc)

ISBN: 978-1-4269-3455-1 (e-book)

Library of Congress Control Number: 2010908822

*Our mission is to efficiently provide the world's finest, most comprehensive book publishing
service, enabling every author to experience success. To find out how to publish your book,
your way, and have it available worldwide, visit us online at www.trafford.com*

Trafford rev. 6/28/2010

North America & international
toll-free: 1 888 232 4444 (USA & Canada)
phone: 250 383 6864 ♦ fax: 812 355 4082

CONTENTS

PREFACE

I wrote this book to keep the memories of history alive, and to use its lessons for a better future.

This book is long overdue. My Father, Bernie Winghart (1900-1997), was involved in bootlegging along with his brother and sister-in-law, Joe and Mayme Schaller Winghart. These escapades and lifestyle were "slightly" known to family and friends for years, and people were curious for more information.

It is time to know all the details and the truth. This book contains reference to many people involved with the era, and I mean no disrespect to anyone caught up in the flow.

I hope you will enjoy the trip through the years with my family as much as I have.

Joan Winghart Wilcox Sullivan

ACKNOWLEDGEMENT

In certain sections of this book there will be some stories written by another author named Scott Wilcox. He was my son, who put several years of part time research in this undertaking. He traveled from Watertown to the Niagara River researching in every library, historical society and lakeshore home that he could gain access to. He made lots of friends. Many hours were spent in newspaper archives, interviewing people and taping interviews on a small cassette player. Scott and his brother Steve, climbed through underbrush, found and crawled into underground tunnels and photographed many areas. Scott loved his Grandfather Bernie, and thoroughly enjoyed talking to all people with stories to tell. Unfortunately Scott (1957-2007) left us before he could complete his bootlegging story, and I will hopefully finish the story so everyone will know how we survived, or not, the Prohibition Era.

Joan Winghart Wilcox Sullivan

CHAPTER 1

"Bernie, You're A Bootlegger"

These words came out of Louise's mouth as she was riding home in a car with her boyfriend Bernie. They had seen a movie at a theater in Niagara Falls, NY and were coming home to the Rochester area. The hour was late and they traveled a dark country road. A vehicle on the road driving towards the couple suddenly crossed the center line and Bernie swerved to the right to avoid a collision. His right arm flew over to hold Louise back in the seat and prevent her from falling forward to strike the dashboard. As the tire went over the edge of the road, the jolt caused a hidden bottle of whiskey to break. The odor was unmistakable.

After Bernie steadied the vehicle, Louise found her voice and she started to give Bernie a tongue lashing about illegal whiskey, when Bernie stopped her saying loudly "That's right sister, but I recommend keeping quiet about it because I'm supplying your Dad with premium quality liquor, or otherwise he would have to drink the rotgut stuff that's being manufactured here in bathtubs (gin) and back yard stills. That stuff can lead to sickness, blindness and even death."

CHAPTER 2

What is this foolish law that turned deadly?

The era of Prohibition was perhaps the most colorful era in the history of the United States, but it also turned deadly, affecting friends, families and neighbors. It troubled the whole country in various ways, but this story will concentrate on one family of thousands who became involved in illegal bootlegging to survive, and also enjoy the challenges and dangers of the game. Bernie Winghart was my Father and he was a bootlegger. He worked alongside his Brother Joe Winghart Jr. and sister in law, Mayme Schaller Winghart. They were sometimes referred to as "The Bootlegging Trio". Many of my family also profited during Prohibition, so I have to admit that "My Family Were Bootleggers."

Congress passed the National Prohibition Act that impacted our country from 1919 to 1932. It was the 18th amendment and often called the Volstead Act after its creator. The act stated that an alcohol content of more than 0.5 % was illegal. It omitted alcohol used for medicinal purposes and sacramental use. The law took effect on midnight 16 January 1920. The restrictions were flagrantly violated by bootleggers and commoners alike. Bootleggers smuggled from overseas and Canada. They stole contraband from the government warehouses, and produced their own booze, Before it came about; there was concern about heavy drinking, causing temperance groups to be formed. These groups became widespread throughout the country and many decided it was time to control the alcohol consumption here, ultimately to reduce crime. Passing the Volstead Act, which stopped legal drinking in the country, was not the answer, but it lasted twelve long, damaging years. Prohibition failed because it promoted gangsters, and crime ran rampant, per example of the Valentine Day Massacre in Chicago, making notorious the names of Al Capone (Scarface), Machine Gun Jack Mc Gurn, and Bugs Moran. There were 136 killings and one conviction in the first five years of prohibition. In 1928, there were 367 murders.

The act brought about a very different lifestyle to our country that included bootleggers, rum runners, moonshiners, smugglers, bathtub gin, speak-easys, back yard stills, booze, roaring twenties and many other new terminologies.

The absence of alcoholic beverages precipitated a large demand for it. Where there is demand there is usually supply. After the law was enacted, thousands of entrepreneurs began devising ingenious ways to supply the parched American people. Living in a border state to Canada, such as New York, there was easy access to Canadian liquor, beer, ale, gin, champagne, and wine. America was exploited during prohibition by Canada and other foreigners like Bill Mc Coy, who was a rum runner from the Bahamas. He would only deal with the good stuff, hence the saying "The real Mc Coy."

Liquor was hidden in hip flasks, false books, hollow canes and many other clever devices. Speak easys replaced saloons. By 1925, there was over 10,000 speak easys in New York. Illegal drinking businesses were controlled by organized gangs. The Bootleg Trio admitted working for the "Black Hand Gang" in Niagara Falls, New York.

In Rochester, there were twice as many speak easys as there were saloons closed by the Prohibition Act. Speak easys were businesses hidden in basements, office buildings, or any conceivable place. You needed a membership or password, and they had alarm systems in place, to avoid being shut down. Arrests for drunkenness and disorderly conduct were surpassed only by arrests for drunk driving.

Bernie always said that his main reason for bringing Canadian whiskey to New York was to save the people. If people drank homemade brews such as bathtub gin or hooch made in back yard stills, they got sick, went blind, or died. Canadian products were very pure to drink. Bernie swore that he saved many people who drank his Canadian products.

America accepted Canadian goods gratefully for a price. Therefore new industries began to appear, though not always legal industries.

1- The transportation industry included boats that could outrun the authorities, and have large storage for booze that could hurriedly be pushed overboard if caught, and boats that could match the gun power of the border patrol boats.

2- Transportation also included automobiles and trucks to run the contraband from the border, or the "dropping off point", to the user or buyer. Secret compartments were necessary along with heavy duty suspension and speed. People no longer wanted four cylinders because they were too slow! Let's give a special mention to horse and buggies and sleighs that the farmers used, to help out when needed.

3- There was a big demand for speak-easys and bars, restaurants, ice cream parlors, hotels, clubs, some under lock and key, that appeared to sell legal goods.

4- We needed more government controls at the border and over the land. Included are officers, larger swifter boats and cars, firepower, and methods of disposing of seized goods. This list could be much longer.

One of the many scams to get goods out of Canada was used by boats of all shapes and sizes. Alcoholic beverages could legally be exported to Mexico, Cuba or a foreign destination. They left Canadian docks bound for Mexico or Cuba with booze, and hours later the same boats returned to the dock for their next legal shipment, and mostly in the dark of night.

Prohibition was one of the most deplorable things that ever happened to America because it caused conflict and hostilities among the people in our country, against each other. When you forbid someone from doing anything, you know what will happen. They will do it anyway. The act put most of the money in the hands of the Mafia in New York City. The gang already controlled prostitution and gambling, and now alcohol. They were not afraid to kill if they had to. The law also made way for homemade brews that made people ill. Feds took bribes that allowed some rich people to stay in business. The results of the Volstead Act were clear. It did not work.

CHAPTER 3

Bernie's Background

Bernie was born 13 September 1900, in an era that was different. It was a time that was unique, a time when most people were solely responsible for themselves and did not blame poor education, non parent involvement, the system, or bad luck for their present or future well-being.

He took responsibility for his own life and lived it to the fullest. Being of the stubborn German descent, he stirred up some people, and others respected and admired his self taught knowledge.

When Bernie was in third grade in a catholic school, his Father, Joseph Winghart Sr. died of tuberculosis. The family lived in a small home in Rochester, New York at the time of Joseph's illness and he was isolated in the attic to protect the children because TB was contagious, with no cure at that time. Bernie's last sad memories of his Dad was knowing that he was dying alone in the attic and feeling very helpless. Joe Sr. left eleven children upon his death; the youngest was two years old. All of the family pitched in and worked as best they could to keep the family strong. Bernie left school in the third grade and helped out at home. He would walk to the Erie Canal bank every day, weather permitting, and pick up loose coal dropped by the barges, and bring fuel home for the stove. The children that were old enough to work ended up as laborers in the shoe factories of Rochester. Bernie had a strong bond with his siblings, especially his brothers because of the loss of his Father.

Leo Winghart, an older brother came home from the war with a steel plate in his head. He was wounded in battle. Leo settled along the shore of Braddocks Bay on Manitou Road in Hilton, New York. Bernie loved to visit him, and at the age of fifteen, he would ride his bicycle from Rochester to see Leo. It was a one way distance of about 20 miles on dirt roads. Sometimes his brother Billy would accompany Bernie and they would ride the Manitou Trolley, which was a shorter route. When they reached the end of the trolley line at Manitou Beach, someone from the Braddocks Bay Hotel would pick them up by boat. Leo lived a few doors from the hotel.

Bernie loved to hunt, fish, and trap while making friends with the area people. He became very good at all those sports, and he was especially fond of the water. Around 1917 he built a "shack" as he called it, on the north side of Braddocks Bay and became a friend of the farmer that rented the land to him. Bernie provided the farmer with fish, ducks, snapping turtles (made great soup) and game. He eventually bought the land and expanded his shack to a home, where I was born.

Then along came prohibition.

Bernie lived weekends at his shack on the bay and spent the week in Rochester with his Mother. He was an adventurer, risk taker, and always looking for financial opportunities, yet he tried to help his Mother and family. He was nineteen years old when talk about bootlegging began to circulate.

If he was to pursue a career in bootlegging, he needed a 'front', or a normal looking career.

Automobiles and motorcycles were just becoming popular and more numerous. At the age of eighteen he bought a Harley Davidson motorcycle. The side car came later. He became a good mechanic out of necessity. His older brother, Joe Jr., was also into vehicles and pursued that career by driving taxi and had part ownership in Seneca Cab

Company in Rochester. He also owned "Winghart's Garage" on Lyell Avenue just off Lake Avenue. These were excellent jobs to cover up their side work of rum running.

When prohibition was in full swing, Bernie lived on Braddocks Bay. His legal address was in Rochester at his Mothers house. His legal occupation was either a mechanic at his brother's garage, or a taxi driver.

CHAPTER 4

Brother Joe and Family

The Winghart family lived in the "Dutchtown" area of Rochester, New York. Dutchtown was in the northwest section of the city loosely bordered on the north and south by Lyell Avenue and West Avenue. Joe and Mayme Winghart spent their early married life there, with a home and businesses. Their life after prohibition was spent between Cape Vincent, NY in the summer and Florida in the winter. After Joe died, Mayme moved back to Dutchtown to live the rest of her life there. Brother Billy Winghart lived, raised a family, and died in Dutchtown.

Joe was more worldly than his brother Bernie. He loved to fish, but did not share Bernie's passion for hunting and trapping. He did however know how to handle a gun, and both Bernie and Joe were good mechanics. Joe was good looking, medium height, had thick dark curly hair and dressed very sharp when he wasn't working or fishing. He was intelligent, good humored and had a fast wit. When they met, Mayme was fifteen years old with long brown hair that reached to her waist. She was very strong willed and knew shortly after she met Joe that he was the one for her. Joe's feeling was mutual and the relationship began. They lived a few blocks from each other in Dutchtown.

Around 1912, Joe was a shoemaker at Leach Shoe Company on 192 Mill Street and lived with his Mother at 2 Duval Place in Rochester. He was dating a beautiful young lady named Mary Schaller but she preferred to be called Mayme. Her mother's name was Mary, and Mayme wanted to be different. She was the daughter of Joe and Mary Koch Schaller. Mayme had five siblings. Two of her brothers ran a very successful restaurant known as "Schaller's". The original restaurant was located on Edgemere Drive near Lake Ontario, and they expanded their business to another restaurant on Ridge Road East and one in downtown Rochester. For a time Island Cottage Hotel on Edgemere Drive was operated by Mayme's sister and brother in law, Almarose and George Reisinger. Through her family Mayme learned much about the restaurant business and shared her knowledge with Joe. This trade would serve them well in their rum running career and after.

The following short story was researched and written by Scott Wilcox, who was Bernie's Grandson. It tells a story about Mayme's Father that illustrates the troubles of the times.

Mayme's Father Joseph Schaller was born about 1876. He shows up in the census in 1894 as a tailor in Rochester. He continues to work as a tailor up to 1919. From 1920 until near his death in 1948, he is listed as a shoe worker and a presser.

SCOTT'S STORY

As a husband and a father, and as in many families that lived in the city during the turn of the century, life could constantly be a struggle. Joseph, with the stress and strain of supporting the family, on occasion would look to the local saloon, to dampen the anxieties that lay upon him. With the excess of one too many drinks and still the thoughts of struggling in the forefront of ones mind, a trip to the saloon can often bring more trouble than relief. This is such the case as on January 28, 1901. Sometime during the evening of the 28th, Joseph, at the approximate age of 25, with his family at home, entered the Balz saloon at 432 Jay Street. An argument broke out with another man as they sat at the bar. What the argument was about is not known. Joseph Holzschuh, a young man of 20 years of age, who argued with Mayme's Father, headed for the door and walked out onto the sidewalk. Right behind Holzschuh came Joseph Schaller wielding a knife. Out of a fit or rage over what was said, the knife went plunging into his back just under the right shoulder blade of Holzschuh. He screamed in agony and before he could defend himself, Schaller pulled the knife out and pitched it in again, this time up high between the shoulder blades. Holzschuh tumbled to the sidewalk with blood flowing from his wounds. John Eckhardt, who was nearby, saw the assault, and interfered to save Holzschuh, and he received a bad gash with a knife wound over his right eye. Louis Holzschuh, a brother of Joseph Holzschuh was in the saloon bartending at the time. When Louis heard his brother's screams, he rushed to his side. Louis hurriedly ran to the nearest phone and called for a doctor. Two other doctors were also called by other witnesses. Sometime between the attack and the time it took for police and medical to arrive, Schaller slipped away and went to his home. Joseph Holzschuh lay on the sidewalk in terrible pain with his brother kneeling beside him. The wound under his right shoulder punctured his right lung and with the loss of blood it was feared he would loose his life. After the doctors arrived he was removed a short distance to his home where the doctors attended to him. The doctors worked feverishly to stop the bleeding and revived him after he lost consciousness.

The police arrived shortly afterwards to take Holzschuh's statement. No reason was given for the attack. He said that he entered the saloon to have a drink and a cigar. He and Schaller had angry words and then he left. At the moment of attack, he turned and recognized Schaller. The police then went to Schaller's house and arrested him. He was then escorted to the patrol wagon and transported to the police station.

It was later reported on March 16 that Schaller was arrested on a bench warrant and charged with 1st degree assault for the stabbing of Holzschuh. How much jail time was served is unknown, but according to census reports, his name was removed from the city directory from 1903 until 1906, when he returned as a tailor again living on Masseth Street, just off Jay Street. Holzschuh, after many weeks of confinement, recovered from his wounds.

End of Scott's Story

In the years leading to Joe and Mayme's marriage, it was a different time for Mayme. She was a typical teenager but she became hardened and resolved to have a good life, due in part and influenced by her Father's incarceration. She dreamed of a better life with money, prestige, and freedom on a grander scale.

After marriage, Joe and Mayme rented an apartment in Dutchtown. In 1917; they purchased a five acre plot along the Orleans County shoreline of Lake Ontario from a farmer named John Martin. This property became their bootlegging haven.

Along came the Prohibition Act.

Joe and Mayme were prime candidates for the bootlegging profession. Joe enlisted his younger brother, Bernie, who was filled with adventure and had a good knowledge of boats and cars.

CHAPTER 5

In The Beginning

The art of bootlegging was not a trade that you could learn in school or anywhere. The one lesson that I have learned over the years is that anyone involved in the trade did not talk! The topic that no one is willing to discuss was mysterious, illegal, sometimes very expensive and often deadly. People were amazingly tight lipped and often carried their secrets to the grave. Those who did talk weren't directly involved, but would not name names. They did not want to embarrass friends or relatives of the bootlegger. Many respected businesses were founded on bootleg money.

Over his 97 years of life, Bernie never talked much about it, or revealed many of the secrets. It was only when he was in his eighties, did he finally speak of it, and only when we badgered him. Then his details were sketchy and we had to dig hard for the truth. By dig, I mean question him, and then get out in the fields, where their houses once stood, and dig to find the underground tunnels. We were successful.

In 1916, Bernie got his first hunting and trapping license. He enjoyed the sports and was just learning, while spending his weekends at Braddocks Bay. At this time, Joe and Mayme Winghart were married and lived in Dutchtown. They had purchased land in Lyndonville, New York on the Lake Ontario shore.

Bernie was a good looking man of slight build in his teens, about 5' 6" in height and weighed about 135 lbs. He had black hair and brown eyes. The one characteristic that you noticed about him was that he moved sure and fast, and was strong and agile. He was famous for his "chair trick". He placed two armless kitchen chairs together facing each other. He would calmly sit in one, straddling it, wiggle and posture for a few minutes to get people nervous, then jump up in the air, turn in the air and end up sitting in the other chair. It made everyone very anxious to watch, but I never saw him miss. Here is where I have to add that Bernie was not a drinker. He took an occasional shot of straight whiskey, but I never saw him drink or have more than one drink at a time.

Around 1920, ideas of making money became mixed with the Prohibition Act in Joe's and Mayme's thoughts. It was a coincidence that they had purchased property on the lake, and Joe was now part owner of the Seneca Taxi Company in Rochester, New York. There were so many ways to profit from the trade, that the Bootlegging Trio started to research the best way to get involved and make the most money. Joe was a very resourceful man, but Mayme's strength of character matched, or surpassed Joe's. They became a formidable couple and Bernie joined them with great admiration and respect for his brother and wife.

In his early 20's, Bernie's transportation was his Harley Davidson motorcycle and he loved tinkering with it. He was a natural mechanic and worked that trade all of his life. He worked for Ford Dealerships in Rochester and in his 60's, repaired small machines for the City of Rochester Garage.

In 1921 Bernie built his first small house, or as he labeled it, a "shack" on Braddocks Bay on the Haslip Tract. He also purchased a sidecar for his cycle to transport his younger brother, or an occasional date. It was in 1921 when Bernie had an accident. He ran off Manitou Road to avoid hitting a car that stopped suddenly. He ended up in a small creek by Burritt Road. His hand got caught in the drive chain, as there were no chain guards then, and removed the ends or three fingers.

His brother took him to St. Mary's Hospital in Rochester and they saved most of his three fingers except for the tips.

When the act first passed, some dealers in alcohol (bars, saloons) held onto their licenses hoping Congress would terminate the prohibition act. By January 3rd, 1920, many had surrendered their businesses. Listed in the Democrat and Chronicle newspaper, many saloons turned in their licenses including the Hotel Seneca, and a business at 319 Central Avenue owned by Pinch and Kleinow. Kleinow was my Uncle. He married my Dad's sister, Marie Winghart. Mr. Kleinow was in the saloon business, but due to Prohibition, he finally moved on to the book binding industry. He was not as adventurous as the rest of the family, although I received many good recipes from him to make homemade wines.

Contraband alcohol started to flow across the border. April 12, 1920, an article stated that it was easy to smuggle across the border from Canada because custom inspectors are far too busy to search for booze. The Prohibition Law was in force, but the government neglected to set aside money to hire people to enforce the law.

Then the raids started.

In May 1920, a couple driving home from an evening at a hotel in Sea Breeze, got into an accident with injuries. This prompted a Sheriffs investigation because the driver was drunk. The District Attorneys Office and the Sheriffs Office used a search and seizure warrant and raided a Sea Breeze hotel. The Geisler Hotel in Sea Breeze was raided by Sheriff Andrew Weidermann, and Deputies Leo Supple and Ray O'Loughlin with Under Sheriff William C. Stalknecht. The confiscated liquor was turned over to a Professor at the University of Rochester to be analyzed. Forty barrels of hard cider was also found.

In June 1920, the Sheriff raided 5 saloons in Rochester with the help of Rochester Police. The saloon of Herbert and Elwood Schulz at 355 Driving Park Avenue is where they seized whiskey. Herbert and Elwood were cousins of my Mother. My Maternal Grandfather, Frank Stortz, ran a bar, grill, and bowling alley on the southwest corner of Driving Park and Lake Avenues. Somehow Grandpa Frank did not get raided, or so he said.

Other relatives of my Mom, Frank H Eyer and Herbert Schulz at 1485 Dewey Avenue were also raided. Two days later, they pleaded guilty to violating the law and were fined $100.00 each, and sentenced to serve three months. In both cases the sentence was suspended.

This was just the beginning of raids, and there was no violence, very few guns and very light reprimands. However as time went on, problems started to escalate.

Another of my maternal relatives was arrested March 1921 at 369 Birr Street in Rochester. Charles Eyer sold two glasses of hard cider to plain clothes agents. He was arrested on a bench warrant.

Other smugglers got creative. On a tip, police raided a Rochester auto garage to discover big five gallon jars, labeled oil, and proved to be whiskey. It was a happy car that got that oil!

My Mother, Elsie Stortz Winghart, had many relatives located in Rochester's Maplewood area. They owned property and were merchants in a variety of goods. Cigar shop, saloons, ice cream parlors, bowling alleys, etc. During prohibition, they devised clever ways to run their business without the sale of alcoholic beverages. Mother's Cousins Edna and Anson Sherman were part owners of a large office building along with Edna's brothers, the Schultz's. It was on the northeast corner of Driving Park and Dewey Avenues. The building housed a dentist's office, music store, grocery and apartments. They still got raided and liquor bottles were found in a safe.

All during prohibition, Mother and Dad were barely acquainted because Bernie vowed he would never marry, while he was in such a dangerous profession. Prohibition ended in 1930. Bernie and Elsie married in 1933, nevertheless, both families were quietly involved.

The Winghart Family's large size included a lot of entrepreneurs. There were Bernie, his brother Joe and wife. Mayme's family, the Schaller's, had restaurants. Brother Billy married Rose Spitz. The Spitz's had a saloon on Edgemere Drive. Sister Marie Winghart Kleinow's husband owned a saloon. Sister Bertha's boyfriend, Nick Hoffman, always had her apartment's bathtub filled with homemade gin! So goes the list of my relatives involved in bootlegging, legal or not.

Some of the devious ways of smuggling across the border were stating to emerge. Smugglers attempted to cross the border and bring whiskey from Canada to the United States. In early 1920, the Canadian government had laws against providing liquor across bars in any way except by government vendor, upon an order from a physician. This

Ontario Province "Dry Law" did not prevent inter- providence traffic by mail or express. Consequently, Americans who wish to take chances, experienced little difficulty having liquor delivered to the US border. Many ingenious devices were used. Auto spare tires were receptacles for wet goods, and partitioned fuel tanks served the same purpose. A hot water bottle made a good whiskey container for the sick. A railroad carload of scrapped iron was sidetracked with whiskey substituted for the iron. On autos, whiskey could be packed in the tonneau cover of the vehicle, rear seats were removed and filled with booze. Many cars were stolen, rear seat areas ripped out, padded with hay, and used to transport booze.

Now that law enforcement was confiscating all types of alcoholic drinks, what did they do with it? For the most part, they destroyed it, but there were small stories that indicated some of the contraband was redirected!

It was called "Breaking of the Bottles". The federal building in downtown Rochester was used to get rid of the confiscated hooch. A story was told of a young boy whose Father was in the Border Patrol. One Sunday morning, Father had to go to the federal building and took his son with him, while his Mother went to church. The basement had a big drain in the floor by a solid wall. It drained into the city sewer system. The men gathered around and threw bottles against the wall to break, as the smelly liquid ran down the drain. The boy was approached by Assistant Marshall Skinner, who said "Hey son, want to have some fun, see if you can break a few bottles." The boy got close to the wall and broke a few. Then the men flushed the debris away with a hose. When he reached home, his Mother said that he smelled like a brewery. She was not happy.

Much of the disposal was done down the sewers into the Genesee River in the raceway behind the jail. It would take around ten trips in a truck to get all the confiscated booze from the warehouse to the sewer. Barrels that were emptied were returned to their owners. Some people, who heard of the dumping, gathered on the river bank, wearing overalls and carrying dinner pails in hopes of catching some of the liquid. The fish in the river fared far better than the people. On April 26, 1922 they dumped 659 bottles of whiskey, 1500 bottles of home brew, 25 large whiskey bottles, wine, hard cider, gin, 2 barrels of hooch, 1 case of wine of pepsin, 83 seven ounce bottles of cider, many pints of cider, and 3 whiskey stills. When it was over there were heaps of broken glass and an odor remained.

Elsie and
Bernie Winghart

Elsie and Bernie's
Wedding day

Bernie Winghart

Bernie at the helm on
St.Lawrence River

Bernie at Beadle Bay

Bernie camping

Agile Bernie

Bernie with
Lulu Martin
and her Mother

Bernie and
Mary Fraser

Bernie's Harley

Bernie's Harley

Bernie and Elsie's cottage
at 1000 Islands

Bernie's shack on
Braddocks bay

Betty and the
boathouse

The cottage

DEPARTMENT OF RAILWAYS AND CANALS

LET PASS

No. 1110

This is to certify that

Ship _Yacht 1012_ .... From Port of _Port Colborne_ .... to Port of _Wilson N.Y._

Official Number _Noxe_ .... Draft _1_ feet _6_ inches.

Carrying cargo listed below has complied with all the Canal Regulations and is entitled to passage through this Canal.

A regular Ship's Report bearing the above number has been duly filed at office shown below.

Vessel	Registered Tons	Country of Origin	Class 2	Tons	Country Origin	Class 3	Tons	Country Origin	Class 4	Class Pr	Tons	Country Origin
Canadian Steam	1		Brought forward			Agricultural Implements	28		Pulpwood	36		
Canadian Sail	2		Hay	16		Cement, Bricks, Lime	29		Sawed Lumber M ft. B M.	37		
United States Steam	3	2 145	Other Mill Products	16		Household Goods and Furniture	30		Squared Timber, M ft.	38		
United States Sail	4		Fruit and Vegetables	17		Iron, Pig and Bloom	19		Shingle, M ft.	39		
Class 5		Revenue	Potatoes	18					Other woods	40		
Passengers			Live Stock	19		Iron, Steel, all other	30		Total, Class 4			
Class 2		Revenue Tons	Poultry, Game and Fish	20		Iron, Steel, all other	30					
Barley	5		Dressed Meats	51		Petroleum and other oils	31		Class 6		Tons	Country Origin
Buckwheat	7		Other Packing-house Products						Hard Coal	41		
Corn	8		Hides and Leather			Sugar	32		Soft Coal	42		
Oats	9		Wool						Coke	43		
Rye	10		All other animal			Salt	33		Copper Ore	44		
Flax	11		Total Tons Class 2						Iron Ore	45		
Peas	13					Wine, Liquors and Beverages	34		Other Ore	46		
Wheat	13	Revenue				Merchandise not enumerated	35		Sand, Gravel and Stone	47		
Flour	14								Total, Class 6			
Total						Total Class 5			TOTAL OF CARGO	48		

I, ... Master, do hereby declare that the above is a true statement, and that my cargo, as reported on Original Ship's Report, is intact and the same as carried when filing Original report.

.... Master.

DIRECTIONS

This report must be signed by the Master of the Ship and delivered to the Statistical Officer at the last office on the Canal, or if using a second canal, at the first office on the next canal, who will forward it to the Dominion Bureau of Statistics.

To DOMINION BUREAU OF STATISTICS

as Ship's Report

by .... No. ....

Stamp of Office using this Let Pass as a Ship's Report

Bernie and Elsie's home
on Braddocks Bay

The Kittenburg Barn on
Curtis Road in Hilton

Joan Sullivan & Scott Wilcox

One of Joe's boats

Joe at Boldt Castle Mayme at Boldt Castle

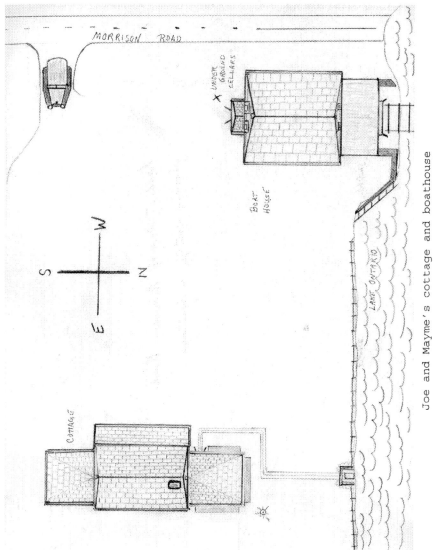

Joe and Mayme's cottage and boathouse

Mayme and Joe's
wedding

Joe and Mayme at
Island Cottage

Joe Schaller
Mayme's Father

Joe's tow truck

Last trip past Stutson Bridge for the ferry

Mayme+Joe

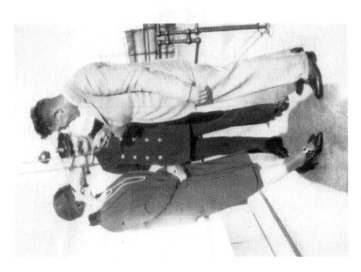

Mayme+Joe aboard the
Ontario Ferry With
the Captain

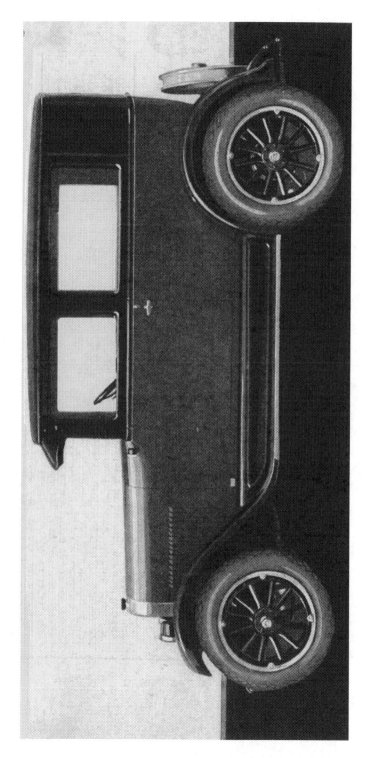

for Economical Transportation

CHEVROLET

Six Cylinder Smoothness

From the very day of its announcement, The Outstanding Chevrolet of Chevrolet History has met with enthusiastic approval in every section of the country—for it combines, to a greater degree than any other car in the world, beauty—performance, —economy—and low price.

Its big six-cylinder valve-in-head motor provides that ample reserve of power so necessary for driving over heavy roads and steep hills. It operates with delightful six-cylinder smoothness and freedom from "lugging"—due to the finer inherent balance of its six-cylinder design. It handles with that effortless ease and safety which can result only from a full ball-bearing steering mechanism and non-locking quiet four-wheel brakes—with separate emergency brakes. Its operating efficiency is so pronounced that it delivers better than 20 miles to the gallon of gasoline! And its marvelous new bodies by Fisher offer outstanding beauty, delightful comfort and rugged hardwood and steel construction—a combination not offered in any other low-priced car.

Here, in short, is an automobile whose power, strength, endurance and economy meet every driving requirement—and whose remarkable *six-cylinder smoothness has never before been available in the price range of the four!*

Visit your Chevrolet dealer today and see this remarkable car. Go over it carefully—from the new six-cylinder valve-in-head engine to the marvelous new bodies by Fisher. Every detail will strengthen your conviction that here is the world's greatest value in an automobile today!

CHEVROLET MOTOR CO., DETROIT, MICH.
Division of General Motors Corporation

The COACH	$595		
The Roadster	$525	The Convertible Landau	$725
The Phaeton ..	$525	Sedan Delivery	$595
The Coupe	$595	Light Delivery Chassis ...	$400
The Sedan	$675	1½ Ton Chassis	$545
The Sport Cabriolet	$695	1½ Ton Chassis with Cab	$650

All prices f. o. b. factory, Flint, Michigan

Bernie packin' pistol

Mayme packin' pistol

41

S.S. Ontario, Cobourg, Ontario.—33.

POST OFFICE AND CUSTOMS OFFICE, MALONE, N.Y.

Steve Wilcox photographing inside
of underground passages

Winghart Hotel
Left Joe   Right Earl

Firemen find saving the "one-time Winghart speakeasy" an impossible job.

Mayme in left rear
Joe in right front
with customers

CHAPTER 6

We're Having Fun

The large parcel of land in Lyndonville, New York was a dream project for Mayme and Joe. The land was at the northern most end of Morrison Road on Lake Ontario. It was a farmer's lane / dirt road for about a mile from the first main crossroad, named Lake Shore Road. At this crossroad they later purchased an old farmhouse and land. The farmhouse was converted into Winghart's Grill. There was a schoolhouse on the opposite corner!

Their first major building project was their summer home, a small one story house with an enclosed porch. Joe had many talents and it was a well constructed wood building, set back from the road and waterfront. Included in the landscape were flowers, dog coop, and very sturdy clothes poles with lines. Of course there was a back storage shed. It was painted white and the neighbors were naturally curious. One lady was heard to tell, after a visit, that the inside was furnished like a palace with beautiful curtains and furniture. Mayme was a master at luxurious surroundings and certainly did not decorate with farmhouse décor. She could also dress like a princess, but when she had work to do she could dress up in a fancy white blouse with pants, boots, and a revolver in a holster on her hip. Mayme meant business. When she made booze runs to Rochester in a new 6 cylinder Chevy, the revolver was under the seat next to Joe's rifle. I feel sorry for any liquor hijacker that tried to stop Mayme. Although she did not look like a typical rum runner with her young daughter sitting on the seat beside her, she supplied many happy buyers in Rochester.

Delivering whiskey to Rochester was safer than making runs to Niagara Falls. Bernie made the Niagara trips. Joe bought two new six cylinder Chevrolets from the Beers Dealership in Medina, New York. He registered one car in Bernie's name and the other in Mayme's name. The springs were built up in the cars to accommodate around ten cases of liquor in the rear, with at least seven inches of space between fender and tire, so passing lawmen would not stop the car. Troopers use to sit on hotel porches in small towns like Murray on Route 104. They watched for heavy loads and then pursued them in their patrol cars.

In the early 1920's, the trio helped distribute good whiskey to many different buyers. Bernie told me they dealt exclusively with liquor. Beer and ale were not smuggled by them because there was not enough money for all the weight carried. Whiskey bought more money per pound. Lifting and moving the goods was physical labor.

The procedure for Bernie's deliveries to Niagara Falls was usually "the dating game." He had two girlfriends that he regularly took to the movies. One girl was Louise Pilon and she did not know that Bernie was a bootlegger. Bernie would get his car loaded with whiskey, then go to Walker, New York and pick up Louise. They rode to Niagara Falls on Route 104, and pulled into a gas station near the theater, then left the keys with the station attendant. After the movie, they would go to a hotel nearby to eat, and come back to the gas station to pick up the unloaded car, and went home. Everything worked beautiful for about a year. Then, on one trip with Louise, when Bernie picked up the keys, the guy at the station said that no one came to pick up the liquor, and Bernie was to return the following night.

On the way home with Louise, and a load of liquor, someone driving towards them must have fallen asleep and crossed the center line of the road. Bernie swerved right for the ditch and the right front wheel cleared a gravel pile, but the right rear caught the pile causing the car to jump and break a bottle making a liquor odor.

Louise realized immediately, and said "Bernie, you're a Bootlegger." Louise started to give Bernie a tongue lashing about illegal whiskey, when Bernie stopped her, saying loudly "That's right sister, but I recommend keeping quiet about it because I'm supplying your Dad with premium quality liquor, or otherwise he would have to drink the rotgut stuff that's being manufactured here in bathtubs (gin) and back yard stills. That stuff can lead to sickness, blindness and even death."

Bernie took her home and broke off their relationship. A few days later Louise came to Bernie's place of employment to make things up. Bernie's boss came into the shop and said that there was a girl to see him. He peeked through the door, saw Louise, and asked his boss to say that he had gone out. A few days later Louise and her Mother came to Bernie's home on Braddocks Bay. He quickly jumped into a rowboat, rowed into the marsh, and hid until they left. Bernie did not need any complications because of his illegal occupation. In 1927, Louise married, and moved on with her life without Bernie.

The trio worked with the "Black Hand Gang" from Tonawanda, New York near Buffalo. The origins of "the gang" started in New York City in the early 20th century. New York City was the second largest Italian immigrant city in United States. The gang was a group of extortionists who ruled by threats and were fueled by the example of the mafia. Their name came about because they sent threatening letters signed with a Black Hand symbol.

An example of their methods showed up in Rochester in 1923. A Mr. La Placa disregarded his "last warning" to contribute $1000.00 to the Black Hand Society. A bomb was exploded in his cellar window at 11 PM one night. The bomb was of the same material used in a previous bombing a week before. It was fashioned of powder, dynamite, scrap iron and paper all wrapped with adhesive tape. Mr. La Placa told police he had received three letters written in Italian. Results of the bombing were broken windows, and walls of the rooms on the lower floors were studded with scrap iron. As far as I know, Bernie had no problem with the Black Hand Gang because they had a good business relationship.

After the summer cottage was built on Joe's land, they were in need of a boat house. The shoreline of Lake Ontario had some good storms, and a boat could take a beating if left near the shore. A good rum runner boat needed a safe place. In the northwest corner of the lot they built the boathouse bordered by the dirt road and the lake. This was a two story home with an open basement underneath to store the boat. Lots of cement was used, and it had more square footage of living space than their summer house. Although this was called a "boat house" it had a kitchen and living room on the lower floor, and two bedrooms upstairs. They needed the height so a light could be placed high in the window to guide their boat at night. The entrance had a domed vestibule added, with a solid concrete floor and concrete step into the house, utilizing two front doors. This house is where Bernie slept when he came to visit, and where Mayme hung the signal light to guide the boat, if the coast was clear.

The construction of this house was so pleasing to Bernie, that he duplicated it on his land at Braddocks Bay. When Bernie built his house on the bay, it was at the same time they were dismantling the Manitou Beach Trolley trestle, so he used some of the strong beams from the trolley for his houses foundation.

The boathouse had another special and unique feature. It contained the entrance to an underground tunnel and storage area lined with cement. No one ever found this tunnel until about 1990, after both houses were torn down by the owner at the time, Rochester Gas and Electric Corporation. People talked and speculated about the tunnels for years. One rumor had it running from the lakeshore to the Winghart Grill. Joe and Bernie were good, but not that good.

To access the steps underground, you used the vestibule. The concrete floor could be raised up. There was a specially constructed hidden winch above the ceiling of the entry, and it raised the concrete floor to allow people to use the ladder to descend. There were two large underground storage areas and a short tunnel that ran toward the cottage. Scott and Steve Wilcox, Bernie's grandsons, did some excavation at the site in 1990 and discovered some of the tunnels and storage areas. Some of the ground was collapsing. They took photos and did some drawings to map out the "bootlegging complex". They also found the metal tracks that were used to pull the boat from the water into the boathouse. There was no tunnel found leading to the Winghart Grille.

Now that their "base camp" was set up, it was time to scout the best way to make money. Joe purchased a Chris Craft with two liberty airplane engines in it. The surplus from the recent war included a lot of liberty engines that were high tech for the era and were water cooled, making them readily adaptable. The engines worked well in a rum runner and were easily converted. The most popular boats used were Chris Craft, Garwood and Hackercraft. Hackercraft manufactured their own engines. The boats that were used depended on what type of water they were running on, and what type of load was being carried. Boats were usually 28 to 30 foot in Lake Ontario, but 20 to 25 foot ran better in the Saint Lawrence River. These were the average style boats used, but many people got creative. A well known bootlegger, Midge Staud, had a boat with heavy copper around the water line so it would not be cut by ice. Ice on Lake Ontario was a real hazard, and would cut through any wood. The Staud Brothers also had a machine gun mounted on their boat. It was rumored that a few people used sailboats to carry contraband. It certainly would not draw the Border Patrol's attention as quickly as a fast speedboat would.

From our area in New York State, there were a lot of creative ways to get whiskey across the border. Our Bootlegging Trio spent time exploring those ways. In the summer of 1923, Mayme, Joe and Mayme's Mother (Mrs. Schaller) and Bernie vacationed at Lake Champlain and Lake Titus. I also have a lovely photo of Joe and Mayme sitting in front of Boldt Castle at the Thousand Islands. This was the beginning of their long term love for the Islands. These vacations were great getaways, while they were scouting for connections and ways to serve New York with fine Canadian liquor.

They found one relatively inexpensive way to not risk losing their own boats or vehicles. Joe and Mayme were the brains and money of the operation and young Bernie did the work gladly because he liked the challenge. Bernie booked a one way passage on the Ontario I or Ontario II Ferries from Rochester to Coburg, Canada.

Here is Scott's story about the ferries.

"Sixty-five to seventy years ago you could take a whole day cruise on Lake Ontario from Rochester to Cobourg, Canada, and back for $1.25. Excursions were run four days a week from downtown Rochester to Cobourg, and back via the B.R. and P. Railroad, and the steamers Ontario I and Ontario II. Boarding the train at the station on West

Main Street in Rochester, you are transported to the Genesee docks near Charlotte, where you are able to board the ship. The prime purpose of these ships was the transportation of coal across the lake, and the ships were called "car ferries" as they had railroad tracks on the lower deck, and railroad cars loaded with coal were put aboard for regular runs across the lake to Cobourg. The upper decks were for passengers, and there was a promenade deck for sports and dancing. Breakfast was provided for only 50 cents, and a dinner for 75 cents. If that was too expensive for you, you could bring along your own box lunch. The first trip across the lake to Canada was made in 1907, and in April 1952 the Ontario II steamed past the upraised arms of the Stutson Street Bridge for the last trip."

When Bernie arrived in Cobourg, he met two Canadians in a 26 foot fast boat with liberty engines. The boats were loaded with whiskey. They traveled at night with no running lights. The Canadians piloted the boat in Canadian water, and Bernie drove in American waters. They landed at various places in US waters. If you did the same route regularly, you would get caught.

One story that Bernie related about the Cobourg trips was a run that he made from Canada to his home area of Manitou Beach. At one time Bernie made the whiskey drop on a long pier that ran from Wiedman and O'Loughlin's Hotel. Bernie and the whiskey got out on the pier in the dark of night and were met by Joe, and helpers in cars, to transport the whiskey. The Canadians went back to Cobourg in their boat.

Others were not so lucky. In August 1923, five hundred cases of Canadian ale were seized in a raid made at the resort of Manitou Beach. In addition to the wet goods, three motor vehicles were taken. There were no arrests! When the officers approached, a shot was heard, and when they arrived at the beach, only wet goods and vehicles were found. All participants had fled the scene.

Some trips came out smoothly and others, not so much. Bernie and Joe were always sure to leave some refreshments for the hotel owners.

CHAPTER 7

North Country, etc.

The fine art of bootlegging was practiced in many ways. Early in the game, territories were established. It was never publicized, but if you were caught delivering contraband in someone else's area, there were often distasteful consequences. The Staud Brothers firmly established their territory in the Rochester area. They were four powerful brothers who came from a well known local family. Their Father was Postmaster for Rochester for a few terms.

Bernie and Joe respected the Staud's "squatter's rights" and were very careful about any activities in Rochester. The Bootlegging Trio was only a very small operation, so they were of no threat to the Staud's. Another factor in determining where they should do business was Bernie's respect for Al Skinner. Al was a Deputy Marshall and lived with his family at Manitou Road, on Braddocks Bay. He and Bernie were friends, and Bernie did not want to upset Al by bringing booze into Braddocks Bay. He did sneak a little in here and there, but he was very careful. Bernie would occasionally take some whiskey for friends, up Salmon Creek to Kittenberg's barn on Curtis Road. He also made a few stops at Manitou Beach.

The territorial game motivated Joe and Bernie to scout out even more places to work, but most of their operation was around Lyndonville to the Niagara/Canadian border.

In the early 1920's, news spread daily of rum running capers that were happening. In March of 1922, a 42 year old Rochester man died at home as a result of drinking poison hooch. The man was out all night at a party and came home drunk. He went to bed to "sleep it off" and in the afternoon complained of feeling sick. In the evening they summoned the ambulance, but too late to save him. The police were trying to locate the source of bad alcohol. In May of 1920, wood alcohol poisoning caused the death of a 19 year old youth from Albion, NY.

Booze generated during this era was generally inferior. Many alcohol concoction seizures that were made by authorities and analyzed, generally proved to be cheap imitations of the real article, done up in fancy containers. Some was plain alcohol, diluted with water that was colored and flavored. To produce gin they used a little juniper sauce. Despite the poor quality, there was a ready market, and many people were sickened or killed from the lethal ingredients.

It was announced that the Prohibition Department had a conference with the Enforcement Department and decided to use more agents and fast motorboats from Chicago to the Atlantic Coast to attempt to stop the smugglers. A month later the government announced that they were "turning the screws" on rum runners in the North Country of New York. When they were asked if the government had a plan to erect block houses along the border with mounted guns, the reply was "Our men carry guns and they know how to use them." A month later the North Country had new warfare to control smugglers. A fleet of approximately 24 Army trucks arrived with mounted machine guns of a light field. We need to remember that most of these rum runners are friends and relations, who are now facing machine guns.

The "North Country" was a term to describe upper New York State. This loosely included the St. Lawrence River and the border area between United States and Canada that stretched to Lake Champlain. Some of the high profile or traffic areas of the North Country prohibition era were: Rousses Point, Malone, Massena Springs, Watertown, Saranac Lake,

Cape Vincent, Clayton, Alexandria Bay, Morristown, Ogdensburg, and Oswego.

Hot spots in the rest of New York State were: Oak Orchard, Lyons, Tonawanda, Sodus, Wolcott, Rochester, Schenectady, Medina, Lakeside, Point Breeze, Lyndonville, and Lockport.

Since we find the Trio spent much time "vacationing" in the North Country, it is safe to assume that they got involved in a profitable business in that area. A greater amount of their rum running was mostly done in the Rochester and the Niagara area. Statistics were released on January 4, 1922 from the Customs officials in Rousses Point, New York for the year 1921. Recorded were 117 liquor laden automobiles seized, 18 liquor laden horses and rigs, and 2000 cases of liquor were also confiscated.

A statement made in April 1922 by a rum runner from Malone, New York swears he never carried a gun. He said that thugs and gunmen run liquor down to New York City, but those carrying contraband to Western New York points are of a "much higher class" hence no need for firepower.

In August 1922, police confiscated three thousand dollars worth of whiskey plus some ale as they raided Cussard's Place, internationally known because of its unique location directly on the US / Canadian border. It was raided by custom agents of both countries. Each worked on their side of the house. United States agents seized fifty quarts of beer and three quarts of whiskey, and Canadian agents seized 300 quarts of beer and 85 of whiskey. The owner, Homer Cussard, was arrested and arraigned.

A statement made in April 1923, stated that the New York and Canadian borders are a "moist place". The chief prohibition agent inspected the border and there were 11 agents guarding 50 roads across the border, where there should be 50 men. We have 200 men in New York City where we need many times that number. There are only 2800 prohibition agents in United States compared to 12,000 policemen in New York alone. Congress needs to appropriate the money to buy the necessary boats and hire men. He found custom agents in United States and Canada all willing to cooperate, but are lacking the fast autos and other equipment necessary, including wireless. He also found that rum runners were observing all Canadian laws possible, but were evading United States laws.

On August of 1925, in Malone, New York, 11,060 bottles of booze were found being smuggled in a freight car, and a week before, 10,000 bottles of liquor were concealed in a freight car shipment of wood pulp. All booze was destroyed. For the month of June 1927, Malone agents seized 33 cars and 75,000 dollars worth of booze. During August 1928 in Malone, a fleet of five cars were captured with 10,000 dollars worth of confiscated items.

Meanwhile, in the St. Lawrence River area, it was an entirely different method of bootlegging and capturing bootleggers. The river was much narrower than Lake Ontario and a fast skiff of Canadian booze could zip back across the Canadian border line, and not be easily caught. The river was treacherous with shoals and shallow places, and a boater that was not familiar with the rivers depths could easily run aground.

It was even reported that some ambitious wintertime smugglers would bring contraband from Canada to United States on ice skates. It was a cold and treacherous trip when you could only carry a few bottles and sometimes a few more on a small sled with runners or skis.

Most of the population of upstate New York Indians also became involved. They carried wet goods across the river in small boats. Many local farmers also provided hiding places in their barns and storage sheds for whiskey and booze laden cars.

An unusual seizure happened just outside of Watertown, New York near Three Mile Bay. Border Patrol seized a "bread truck", a new 1928 Reo Speedwagon disguised as a United Bakers bread truck with 75 cases of Canadian ale valued at about $750. The truck was valued at $2000. The beer was Black Horse, Red Cap, Dows, Frontenac, Queens, and Labatts ale.

The St. Lawrence River captured Joe and Mayme with its beauty and later they settled there. During 1923, Beadle Bay in Cape Vincent was a rendezvous of smugglers. This is where Joe and Mayme later bought land. After they bought land and built their summer cottage, Elsie and Bernie also built near them.

CHAPTER 8

Things Are Heating Up

In 1923, Joe decided to phase out of his taxi business in Rochester and formed his own business called "Winghart's Garage". It was located on Lyell Avenue in Rochester, on the northwest corner, one building from Lake Avenue.

The taxi business became somewhat dangerous for Joe. In April he was assaulted by four men in a yellow cab, after being forced to the side of the road. Four men alighted and struck him with short pieces of iron pipes. A customer in Joe's cab escaped to summon help, but Joe's assailants fled in the cab before police arrived. There was a trial, and it seemed there was some sort of labor dispute among taxi drivers.

Joe must have considered driving a cab unsafe and concentrated his talents on the automobile repair industry. He did quite well, and had a noteworthy tow truck for road calls. Tow trucks were just coming in "vogue" and Joe's was specially built. At that time a tow truck was more of a "service truck." The main goal was to repair the broken down vehicle on site, and towing it to the garage as a last resort. Bernie used to tell stories of laying on his back in snow, rain and mud under a car to repair it.

1924 was a memorable year for Joe and Mayme. They had a brand new legitimate business and they adopted a little girl who they named Betty. Their side business of bootlegging slowed for a year or so, but picked up rapidly again in 1926.

During the mid 1920's the Coast Guard was given a general order to work in conjunction with federal authorities. They were to keep their eyes open for boats that may be engaged in rum running and take action that would result in a seizure. This included Lake Ontario Coast Guard stations at Big Sandy, Oswego, Charlotte, and Niagara. (Niagara Coast Guard picked up Joe and Bernie). The Coast Guard was to record comings and goings of small and large boats. To prove that the Coast Guard was serious, on June 1, 1925, armed with an arsenal designed to strike terror into the hearts of rum runners, the new patrol boat, CG143, arrived at the Summerville station. It was 75 feet, 12 ½ beam, with a 37 mm gun on the forward deck. It fires three one pound shots a minute. Also added was a machine gun that fires 100 shots a minute. It carried an eight man crew, each equipped with an automatic revolver and an army rifle. The boats new skipper was Stanley J. Kullowski. To illustrate the corruption during the times, Skipper Kullowski lasted from June 1, 1925 to August 21. He was suspended for negligence in his duties which involved permitting certain smugglers to carry on without Coast Guard intervention.

Before his suspension they did however, capture smugglers at Nine Mile Point and seized on land one Selden Truck valued at $2200, with less than 500 miles on its speedometer. Also confiscated were one Oldsmobile truck valued at $600, one Cadillac touring car at $500, one Studebaker touring car valued at $1700 (It is unusual that a Studebaker was worth more than a Cadillac), 400 to 500 cases of ale at $10,500 to $11,000, and a four ton Cabin Cruiser, 36 foot long, valued at $2000 to $3000.

The Border Patrol had to devise a way of handling their confiscated goods. In Rochester, the confiscated vehicles were funneled to a two story cement building on Averill Avenue near South Avenue. The building was equipped with an elevator to handle large cars. Vehicles were stored on the second floor, while on the first floor they were repaired and serviced. The vehicles were sometimes used by the Border Patrol, but most were auctioned off. At times bootleggers bought back their own cars, or it went to the highest bidder. A similar procedure was used for seized boats.

There were more bootlegging hoaxes being reported in the Rochester area. Rochester police found a car in a garage on Joseph Avenue and Ward Street loaded with dolls. The Police Captain opened a case of dolls to find twelve bottles of gin. Another case of dolls revealed a dozen bottles of scotch. A car of dolls turned into over $1000 of gin and scotch. Officers confiscated the car, dolls and contents.

A fire did considerable damage to a garage at Ajax and Tallinger Alleys exposing a bootlegging operation. Found were 1200 bottles of Buffalo Beer, 30 gallons of alcohol and two 30 gallon stills. The Police are looking for the owners. Federal agents came from New York City to investigate. They questioned the owners, who were Park Avenue residents. They sublet the property to Mr. Kling. When Mr. Kling was questioned, he said that he had rented the place to two strangers whose names he did not know. When he rented the building, the strangers said they were doing chemical experiments?

Back in Orleans County, the rum running business was also becoming more involved. There was a new Sheriff on the horizon. A newspaper article stated that Ross Hollenbeck of Albion, who was Undersheriff of Orleans County for five years, announced he was running for Sheriff's Office. His wife possesses all the qualities required on behalf of a sheriff's helpmate, who is called upon to act as Matron of the Jail.

He was elected Sheriff and became very active in trying to control rum running activities.

A talk with Sheriff Hollenbeck's brother, Fay, in later years showed insight into the Sheriff's challenges in the county where the Bootlegging Trio lived. Ross was voted to office during the Prohibition Act to a county with a lot of Lake Ontario water frontage. His responsibilities were chasing, arresting and confiscation goods like alcohol, vehicles, horse and buggies, boats and whatever. Big boats would run as close to shore as they could, and row boats would unload the goods on the shore or pier. The farmers became involved with horse and buggies to draw goods to their barn. Barns stored booze until it was distributed.

Vehicles were stored in barns also. In cold weather the cars were stored as near as they could to the warm cows, so radiators would not freeze. The cars often smelled of cows and barns.

The sheriff had to wait until bootleggers unloaded because he had no boats to catch them. Deputies usually hid and watched until the barn was loaded and then moved in. The people in boats, who never came ashore, were free.

Whiskey bottles were usually in a cardboard protective case (corrugated wrappers) with twelve bottles to a burlap bag. The cheaper version was straw. Sometimes there were eight to ten bottles per bag, to make them lighter to handle.

Sheriff Hollenbeck kept the confiscated horses on his brother's farm until he sold them or auctioned them off.

Brother Fay Hollenbeck transported the confiscated wet goods for his brother the Sheriff. He took it from Albion to the Rochester Post Office downstairs basement. The head of the Post Office was a man named Staud and his son was a main bootlegger. On the drive from Albion to Rochester with his truck loaded with illegal booze, he had four or five police cars ahead of, and behind, so he wouldn't be hijacked. He had a police escort all the way.

Sheriff Hollenbeck became acquainted with Bernie in a frightening way. One summer night, Bernie came upon a road block. He was coming out of Point Breeze in his 6 cylinder Chevrolet with a load of whiskey. He turned from a dirt road onto a main road (Route 18) to Kuckville. Bernie was at the top of a hill looking down to a roadblock at the bottom by a stream. He noticed that there were two police cars facing him. The officers stood in the road waving their pistols at him, wanting him to stop. It was almost dark and Bernie decided not to stop, but hit the gas pedal, knowing that by the time they turned their cars around, Bernie would be gone. Bernie's words were "I almost killed two police. If they didn't jump out of the way, I would have killed both of them." He ran the road block, turned off all of his lights, and used the hand brake if he had to slow or stop, so his stop lights would not be seen. They did not catch him. However, about a week later Bernie was driving out Route 104 and stopped for gas at a gas station in Gaines. He looked in the open door of the garage and there sat one of the police cars. They were working on it, and one of the guys walked over to Bernie's car. A station attendant was filling Bernie's fuel tank. Bernie sat in the driver's seat, window rolled down, and his arm on the window sill. Ross Hollenbeck tapped Bernie on the shoulder. Bernie had never met him, but the Sheriff knew his name. Hollenbeck said "Bernie, let me tell you something. The next time I get in front of you and you don't stop, I'm gonna shoot you." Bernie replied "Are you through talking?" Hollenbeck nodded. Bernie continued "Well, let me tell you something. Remember two weeks ago when they shot one of the custom guys up at Olcott Beach? If you bother me anymore, I'm working for the Black Hands in North Tonawanda, and they will pop you off just like him." Hollenbeck walked away and never bothered Bernie again.

Other capers were happening in the Lyndonville area where the Trio was based. A bootlegging gang of men in Lockport were arrested for illegal possession of liquor. They were found on a farm near the beach of Lake Ontario. Confiscated was a fast motor boat and liquor worth thousands of dollars. Seized also were two trucks, and two pleasure cars. Arrested were the farm owner, a man from Olcott, and seven men from Buffalo. The illegal operation was turned into police by local farmers complaining of a mysterious boat seen to land on the large pier, and motor vehicles traversed the roads all hours of the night and early morning. The raid was too late to catch the boat which sped away, but just in time to catch the loading operation.

CHAPTER 9

We Got Caught

As the Trio was getting older and wiser, they became more involved in bootlegging. Life was good at the summer cottage in Lyndonville, and everyone became more comfortable with their neighbors. The Martins owned the farm east of Morrison Road, and Joe and Mayme had bought their shore line property from them. The Frasers owned the property on the west of Morrison Road to the lake, and Joe and Mayme bought several acres from them including the farmhouse.

Bernie took advantage of the situation and began dating the farmer's daughter, Mary Fraser. Mary lived in the farmhouse that Joe eventually bought. When Scott interviewed Mary in later years she remembers sitting at dusk with her family at the lakes edge of Morrison Road, and watching Bernie and Joe bring in the boat loaded with whiskey. A familiar sight to the neighbors also was Bernie cruising down the dirt roads in his Harley with the side car.

Bernie soon moved on to date another farmer's daughter, Lulu Martin. She was seventeen when she first dated him and their friendship lasted two to three years. Bernie refused to settle down when he was pursuing his bootlegging career.

Scott talked to Lulu in 1999 when she was ninety years old. Her story was, when Joe bought the land from Lulu's Father, they all became good friends. They made an agreement to store and hide whiskey and cars in the Martin barn. Lulu witnessed nighttime lights flashing between Mr. Martin at the barn, and the Winghart's at their waterfront property. When Lulu asked her Mother about the happenings, her Mother told her not to say anything.

Scott asked Lulu if she knew that Bernie was a bootlegger she had a big smile and replied "Yes, I knew." She also said that Bernie and Joe protected John Martin, doing whatever it took to keep the barn a secret, and keep Mr. Martin free of suspicion from others, and the law. Lulu spoke very well of Bernie and Joe, citing many kind things that they did.

Bernie and Lulu drifted apart because she heard that he was interested in another woman, who eventually became Bernie's wife. Lulu Martin Zimmerman married at the age of twenty-four.

Joe made Bernie Captain of their Chris Craft boat. Regular trips were made to Port Colborne in Canada by way of the Welland Canal. I have a copy of "Department of Railways and Canals LET PASS" from 1929. The pass was signed by the Captain William Hilstorf, alias Bernard Winghart. If I were to choose a fictitious cover up name, it would be Smith or Jones, not Hilstorf! Regardless of his alias, I have a Christmas card sent to Bernie Winghart from a boat captain who lived in Port Colborne. The card had Bernie's proper name and address on it.

During the summer months there was a lot of press talk about the smuggling of booze in large armadas from Port Colborne to United States. Stories appeared in Rochester and Watertown newspapers.

In February 28, 1929, the game warmed up. This article appeared in a local Lyndonville paper.

Liquor Cargo Siezed
February 28, 1929

Alleged liquor smugglers early Monday morning managed to unload a cargo estimated to be worth $3,000 into two expensive automobiles, and to dodge customs border patrolmen in time to "park" the cars in a barn almost a mile from the lake, but failed to reckon with tell-tale tracks made by their tires in the snow.

The trail led from the lake shore four miles west of Lakeside, in the town of Yates, to a barn on a farm owned by John Martin. When questioned by Collector of Customs Andrew Wiedenmann and Deputy Collector Frank Gallagher, Martin disclaimed knowledge of the automobiles and their contents.

In each car, 20 bags of alleged rye and Scotch were found. The seized cars were registered in the names of Bernard and M. A. Winghart, who are said to be owners of a cottage nearby. The customs men have made arrangements to question them as soon as other witnesses have been disposed of. End of article.

We never got the full outcome from this clash with the authorities. We do assume however that the liquor was seized, but the vehicles were not confiscated because the police illegally broke and entered the barn of Mr. Martin. Another first hand account of this incident was heard from Mr. Martin's son Jim (Lulu's Brother). Scott interviewed Jim Martin and his story follows.

Jim Martin

The day the customs men came, they followed the snow tracks right to the barn and broke open the door to get in. They discovered two autos and whiskey. Both autos were large. There was also a third car in the barn that belonged to my older brother, Mike. Whiskey was in the two large cars, but none in Mike Martin's car. After the customs men made the discovery, they proceeded to the Martin house. Joe Winghart would, from time to time, give Mrs. Martin a quart of whiskey. Mrs. Martin would use that quart for medicinal purposes only, mixing it with water and sugar and giving it to the kids when they suffered from illnesses such as whooping cough. As the customs men approached the house, Mrs. Martin poured the quart down the sink.

After police questioned the Martins, John Martin let his anger be known about the customs men breaking open the barn doors before coming to the house and asking first what was in the barn. They went before a judge and nothing much came of it.

Jim Martin does not remember the date, but sometime after the liquor cargo seizure incident, fire erupted one day, on the Martin property just after thrashing grain, and it burned down three of their barns. One barn was where the cars and whiskey were hidden. The cause of the fire was not certain, possibly a carelessly thrown cigarette from the nearby road.

Jim Martin continues reminiscing to Scott about his times with Bernie, Joe and Mayme.

JIM MARTIN

Joe and Bernie built a boathouse near lake level and there was an overhead door with a steel track leading out into the water. A boat could be winched up the track and into the boathouse.

Loads of whiskey would on occasion, come in on an afternoon, but mostly at night. John Martin would help from time to time unload whiskey from the boat and onto a waiting car.

When you entered the front door of the boathouse, there was a trap door in the floor at the entrance area, inside the first door. There would be a rug or some kind of covering over the trap door. There was a pulley and cable over the trap door at the ceiling that was used to pull or drop whiskey into the cellar below. The area in the cellar would hold over 200 cases.

One day when the authorities were there to speak with Bernie and Joe, they stood right on top of the trap door and didn't realize that it was there.

Other nearby neighbors were also bootlegging, but not to the extent that the Trio was. Jim remembers seeing Sheriff Ross Hollenbeck patrol up and down Lakeshore Road from time to time. Jim remembers

Hollenbeck as being nasty. (I guess I would be nasty also, considering the nasty job that the Sheriff had.)

Over the years, this peaceful farming, lakeshore community had turned into a "cat and mouse" game between residents and their elected officials. Prohibition is an era for people to remember and not make the same mistakes. The business brought a new vitality to the countryside at the time, but now many areas stand forgotten, overgrown, and crumbling, or gone.

CHAPTER 10

We Almost Got Caught

The group was quite successful in the later years of the Prohibition Act. They ran into a few more bumps before the end of the era.

Bernie told a story about a mishap on Lake Ontario, that I heard through the years, but I assumed that he embellished the story. Boy, was I wrong!

Scott and I made a trip to the Youngstown Coast Guard Station near the mouth of Niagara River. I was searching for old logs and notes from July 1929, to see if Dad really got picked up by the Coast Guard. About a year and several inquiries later, I received documents from the Coast Guard archives in Chicago, Illinois.

Bernie's version was: "We were running Lake Ontario, coming from Niagara with a load of whiskey. The sun was setting in the west, behind us. We had our big boat with twin Liberty engines and the lake was a little rough. We were out from the Niagara River when I slowed the engines and looked back at the transom. There was sun shinning through the big hole by the propeller. I grabbed my jacket and some rags and dove at the hole to stuff it, while Joe started bailing. We were dead in the water, and a nearby boat saw us in trouble. They came over to us and offered to take us ashore. I was the Captain and I wasn't going to leave the ship. They said that they would go for help. It was getting dark as they left. We knew they would get the Coast Guard, so we started dumping the booze overboard. When the CG picket boats arrived, we were empty of liquor and sinking and bailing. They towed us to land. I stayed in the boat and Joe rode on the Coast Guard boat. They beached the boat on their property and we picked it up the next day."

The Coast Guard version was:

RECORD OF THE MISCELLANEOUS EVENTS OF THE DAY as found in the Coast Guard Log for Friday, July 9 (19), 1929.

4:00 PM to Mid.

Changed lookout clock dial at 4:00 pm. All lookout duty properly performed. Beach patrol was omitted as Picket Boats covered patrol limits. Colors at Sunset. Evening inspection at 8:00 PM, conditions satisfactory. About 8:15 PM, B. M. Bedell received a telephone message from the Canadian Steamship Company that the Canadian Steamer Cayouga had passed a small motor boat with two men in distress about 10 miles N. by E. of station and offered to take men off but men refused to leave boat as motor boat was too frail, it could not be towed behind steamer who upon arrival at Niagara on the Lake reported the incident to this Station. Picket Boats CG2206 and CG2364 were immediately manned and proceeded to scene of accident arriving there about 9:45 PM and found the disabled motor boat 101Z said to be bound from Pt Dalhouise to Toronto Ontario with two men aboard and bent in a sinking condition. Motor boat was towed to this station and hauled out to keep from sinking. This motor boat owned by George Thompson of Buffalo, NY. William Hillstorf Route 2 RFD Lyndonville, NY left Pt. Dalhouise at about 1:30 PM this date and when in the above position discovered boat was leaking water very fast and all articles of any weight were thrown overboard in order to help make the boat as light as possible and if this boat had not been picked up within a very short time the occupants would have been unable to keep her afloat as they had just about given up hope of being rescued and were ready to don life preservers and go overboard as a last chance. Crew returned to station at 11:30 PM.

W.M. BEDELL,
ACTING OFFICER IN CHARGE.

The local newspaper version was:

LYNDONVILLE MEN TAKEN
FROM LEAKY CRAFT IN ONTARIO
JULY 25, 1929

Rescue of William Hillstors, 34, and John Hillstors, 28, Lyndonville brothers, by coast guards on Lake Ontario, eighteen miles northwest of Youngstown late Saturday night, became known Sunday. There was a heavy sea and their speedboat was half filled with water entering through two holes stove in the stern when the coast guards reached them. The brothers were near exhaustion from bailing. The brothers went through the Erie and Welland canals in their speedboat and left Port Dalhousie, Ont. for Toronto, across Lake Ontario. A heavy sea was running. About fifteen miles out they noticed there was considerable water in their boat. Raising the floorboards they discovered two holes had been stove in the stern.

They tried ineffectually to stem the water entering the boat by plugging the holes with rags. They resorted to bailing. They threw every movable object aboard the boat overboard, except two lifesavers. The captain of the Steamer Cayuga bound for Niagara-on-the-Lake from Toronto, offered to pick the brothers up, but hoping to save their craft, they declined the proffered aid.

When the Cayuga reached port, its captain notified the United States coast guard station at Youngstown and two picket boats set out to the rescue, reaching the disabled craft just as the brothers had decided to don the life preservers and jump overboard. The men were taken aboard one of the picket boats and their water-logged craft was towed to the coast guard station. Rescuers and rescued reached the station shortly after midnight. The brothers went home Sunday noting their boat will be repaired at Youngstown.

There was certainly a lot of booze buried in Lake Ontario's bottom.

The boat was repaired, and Joe had it for many years until it was destroyed by a fire in his storage area at Point Breeze.

While prohibition was coming to an end, the Trio had to make a lifestyle change. They devoted twelve years to bootlegging and a covert lifestyle. Now they were free to live a normal life, but what was a "normal life" for them? Mayme and Joe had purchased the Fraser farm and acreage to the lake. Since their expertise was not farming, they converted the farmhouse into Winghart's Grille. Joe knew little about farming, and Mayme knew a lot about the restaurant business. Since their daughter, Betty, was in the local school system, they felt it was a good place to settle.

The grille was very popular and at first it was called a "speakeasie" because they opened their business a little before the prohibition act was repealed.

Jim Martin worked for Joe at the farm and grille for 10 cents an hour, doing odd jobs on the farm such as planting orchards, picking fruit and helping with the restaurant. One time Jim drank too much and got sick. Joe took him out on the back porch and fixed him a tomato concoction that eased his sickness.

Mayme was in charge of tending of the bar. She would water drinks down so she could continue to have drinks bought for her, therefore putting more money in the cash drawer.

Joe had fruit trees and also raised chickens. Joe was not a farmer. He took a great loss on fruit one year and decided to move on. They had already sold several lots along Lake Ontario and now sold the entire farm. The schoolhouse across the corner was empty, so they converted it into a home. They wished to stay in the area because of Betty's education, and they still had their summer cottage on the lake, complete with obsolete underground tunnels and storage.

The fate of the Winghart Grille was that in later years, it burned to the ground. People were very pleased with food and service at the restaurant, during and after, the Winghart's ownership. Later owners were not as meticulous and it became known as a "dive". In the newspaper article picturing the firemen attempting to save the building, the photo caption read, "Firemen find saving the one time Winghart speakeasie an impossible job." Another quote from the article is "The tavern which was closed was reportedly operated as a speakeasie during the prohibition era. Legend has it that an underground tunnel led to a small cottage near Lake Ontario, through which alcoholic beverages were smuggled in from Canada,"

Then, along came an opportunity that suited them very well. They purchased the large hotel on Lake Ontario at Point Breeze. By this time Betty was in high school in Albion, New York and the hotel was convenient to the school bus route. The area had a resort atmosphere and they successfully ran the "Winghart Hotel" for many years. There were rooms to rent upstairs with a bar, kitchen and dining room down. The grounds also had a dance hall and concession stands. Two years after they purchased the complex, a fire burned the dance hall, cottage, two refreshment stands and Joe's treasured rum running boat. They suspected arson, but it was never proved.

The hotel was located on a corner property of Lake Ontario and Oak Orchard Creek, where good fishing brought in the customers. If the fishing wasn't good, the bar was always open.

Bernie moved to his shack on Braddocks Bay, but enlarged and remodeled it, to be almost the same as Joe's boathouse. Of course, there were no secret tunnels. His new wife, Elsie, made the house look like a home. Bernie worked the night shift at Judge Motors on Lake Avenue in Rochester. He was a good mechanic and also took charge of the nighttime towing service. His real passion was hunting, fishing, and trapping, which he did during the day, with a little sleep in-between. The Trio was now split into respective family units of husbands, wives and each had a daughter. They raised their children and reunited in retirement years.

CHAPTER 11

Bernie, You're Amazing

The St. Lawrence River captured Joe and Mayme with its beauty. They loved the water and boating. After the prohibition era, and their next decade of earning a living, they purchased Wedding Cake Island, one of the 1000 Islands. Next they decided that they wanted to winter in Florida, so they purchased a large plot of land from a local farmer at Beadle Bay in Cape Vincent, New York. No doubt they were familiar with this area because it was a local bootlegging hot spot.

They again divided the land into lots along the river and sold parcels. Bernie and Elsie chose the first two prime lots. They built a lovely two bedroom ranch style cottage high above the river. It was close to a dense woods. We do have to admit that there were underground caves in the woods due to the abundance of stone in the area. We never checked the caves for contraband liquor!

Joe and Mayme built a cottage and a matching boat house for the summertime and they wintered in Florida. Bernie and Joe did some fishing together just like they used to.

71

Scott tells the rest of the story: The bootleg trio finally broke up in the year 1968. Bernie and Mayme said their last goodbyes to Joe. It was an unusually mild October day, with their gathering place at the Hauber and Stalknect Funeral Home on 828 Jay Street in the Dutchtown section of Rochester, New York. At age 74, Joe's soul departed this earth to be with his maker. The loss to Bernie and Mayme was worse than dumping a load of good Canadian whiskey to the bottom of Lake Ontario.

Forty years before, during prohibition the trio on a number of trips across Lake Ontario experienced loss and frustration of dumping whiskey overboard due to the Coast Guard hot on their wake. But now the loss of family would hurt much more. Mayme would have to go on without a husband and Bernie without a big brother whom he looked up to and respected.

During the 1920's there was a struggle and a dangerous lifestyle played out, but Bernie as a young man in his prime, bold, cocky and undaunted, would not have lived it any other way.

Ten years after Joe's death, Scott was still impressed with Bernie's ability to handle a boat in a rough trip across the St. Lawrence River. Bernie was 78 years old. Scott's story about him and his Grandfather follows.

It was August '78 right in the middle of the dog days of summer. I had arrived on a Friday night to spend a weekend with my grandparents at their cottage in the 1000 Island region. Saturday morning dawned with warm southerly breezes and nothing but blue sky. After a hearty breakfast put together by Grandma, Gramp and I headed to the pier with all our fishing gear. On the way down, a neighbor yelled out his door, "Hey Bernie, save some fish for me!" We both got a chuckle out of it, but Gramp sure had a reputation about cleaning out a fishing hole.

I handed Gramp all the gear off the pier necessary too make for a half day of fishing. After he laid the poles and the fishing tackle boxes in their proper place, I slowly slid in, not to rock the boat. He always ran a tight ship and while he was Captain, you always obeyed orders or that was your last time out. Our destination today is Bayfield Bay, this bay is home of the large mouth bass. Bayfield Bay is located three and a half miles up river (west toward Lake Ontario), it lays on the southern Canadian shore of Wolfe Island. With everything in place, Gramp fired up the motor of a 45 horsepower Evinrude which propelled his sixteen foot Starcraft closed bow boat. After casting off the bow and stern ropes, we pushed off from the pier and out through Beadle Bay. Gramp always made it a habit that after clearing the weed line in the bay, before reaching the river, he would put the motor in reverse and give it the throttle to blow any weeks off the propeller. As we enter the river, Wolfe Island lays three quarters of a mile straight across from us. Instead of crossing the river in that direction, we turn left from the shelter of the bay, build speed to plane (level the boat), and head diagonally across the river passing to the back side (north side) of Carleton Island, which is an American Island. The wind was picking up some out of the southwest and the river was a little choppy, but it was just beautiful with the sun glimmering on the waves, and us moving like a stone skipping across the water. What a sense of freedom and a feeling like I could just toss my cares away, but little did I know at that time, I would be fearing for our lives later. Would Gramp's skills in handling a boat, as back in the bootlegging and rum running days, come into use today?

The international boundary lies near the southern shore of Wolfe Island, and the international shipping channel is between there and Carleton Island. As we reached the backside of Carleton a 720 foot cargo ship heading down river, passed just moments before, leaving a six to eight foot rolling wake behind. Gramp saw it as a thrill, but after expressing my concern, he eased up on the throttle so we would gently roll into it. After our gentle roller coaster ride we crossed the international boundary into Canadian waters, and within a quarter of a mile entered Bayfield Bay between Wolf Island and Bayfield Island. Gramp knew this bay so well, where the channel was, and how to avoid the weeds from getting caught up in the prop. He slowly eased up to about 500 feet off shore and had me gently slide the anchor in the water. We sat in about six to seven feet of crystal clear water. The bay was beautiful and void of man made noise, but wonderfully boisterous of wildlife. There were occasional sea gulls overhead along with a pesky red winged blackbird, who was trying to make it clear we were near its nest in the cattails. The lily pads were plentiful and green, and in between a couple of white flowers that bloomed in rich nutrients. This bay was also very protected from the prevailing west wind and it was very calm as Gramp prepared his pole. He became busy right away casting his line out in many directions. I was ready to sit back and relax and enjoy my surroundings, but Gramp reminded me to grab the net if he got one on. Within a matter of a dozen throws, he was yelling "grab the net". I netted quite a number of bass, but he was very good at releasing the smaller ones and only keeping the prize one which would be in the seven or eight pound category. During the coming years as Bass Contests and fast bass boats became popular in this region, it became an infringement upon Gramp's favorite fishing spots and this make him quite upset. With the numbers growing of more bass fishermen and contests, it became a big part of the reason why he lost interest in fishing the 1000 Islands in his later years. Fishing was part of his livelihood and it was sad to see that fade away.

After every fifteen or twenty minutes, we would move the boat to a different spot so he wouldn't play out one spot. He kept his focus on the fishing and I, the meteorologist I think I am, kept one eye to the sky.

Weather fascinates me, especially summertime thunderstorms. As long as I'm out of harms way, I enjoy a lightening display and the crashing boomers that come afterwards, though out in a boat on a large body of water, that's another story. After an hour had passed, I noticed to the west in the distance a distinctive line running north and south across the sky, where moments ago, nothing. To the west of the line the color was dark blue, and at that moment it came back to me about the weather forecast that I heard at the breakfast table. A sharp cold front was going to pass through this region and bring heavy downpours, thunder, lightening, and a drop in temperatures. I brought it to Gramp's attention that we may be in for nasty weather; he assured me we wouldn't be here much longer. Before two minutes passed a rumble of thunder brought a realization that this storm was going to move in quickly. I urged him that it was now time to go. Without looking back, but looking down on his line and lure, as he reeled in, he answered "just three more throws", one of his most favorite sayings when fishing. I again scanned the sky, this time the appearance of lightening bolts zig-zagging across the sky and the rumble of thunder becoming louder and more frequent, was raising my level of urgency to leave as soon as possible. After more than three throws were cast, I again pressed him, but those four words I heard again, "just three more throws." This time my eyes were glued on him and not on the storm knocking on our back door. After his third throw, while he was reeling in the line, with my voice now trembling I said "okay Gramp, that's enough" and I immediately reached over the side and pulled in the anchor. "Hey!, take it easy, how am I going to catch fish with you jumping all over the boat?" I blurted back, "Gramp, I really enjoy being out here, but not with this storm coming upon us." Okay, Okay! Let me put the pole away and we'll get going". As the pole was put away, he told me that this wouldn't be the first time he experienced rough weather and assured me that we would make it back in fine shape. So there was no need to get all excited. The dependable Evinrude started right up and we slowly throttled out of Bayfield Bay. Again as we reached the edge of deep water, he kicked into reverse and threw the weeds off the propeller. A couple of large drops stated to land on us. Before we took off across the river, he reasoned the wise thing to do would be to put the canvas top up to keep us somewhat dry. I have never been fishing with him before that we had to raise the canvas. This would be our first storm together and our last. At this point in my life my back was turned to the Lord my God and Savior, whom is really in control of all things. But since my back was turned, I put my life into Gramp's hands. Through the power and the will of God, Gramp did a great job and I compliment him today for keeping a cool head and acting low key about the seriousness of this situation, this was no time to panic.

With the canvas up and everything tied securely down, we quickly broke plane and headed east. The rain drops grew in size and came down at a faster rate, our sunny morning was turning into a turbulent storm as the cold front would soon overtake us. Gramp reached for the windshield wiper switch. It became impossible to see through the windshield as it was now pouring. We cleared Carleton Island and entered open water, though my peripheral vision off the port side, I saw a passing freighter, but other than that, we appeared to be the only ones out there. At this time I wasn't out here to count boats. From here on in, I was looking straight ahead over the bow towards our destination, home port. We were still about two miles from Beadle Bay, when a heavy fog settled down on the river. I glanced to my left (north) and could not see Canada, I glanced to my right (south) and could not see the U.S. A sense of panic set in me very quickly; as my voice trembled I asked Gramp how will we ever make it back? In an assuring voice he turned to me and said, "You forget who I am. I'm a clever sea captain with this compass in front of me, and we will make it home in time for lunch." I was still scared, but my panic level dropped after his reassuring words. As suddenly as the fog set in, within a half mile the wind came on in a rage. From what direction, I did not know. The boat was being tossed around and it was pouring so hard, I thought the canvas was going to rip wide open. Thunder and lightening was a continual display. One good thing was, with all the commotion, the fog lifted somewhat and improved the visibility. In fear of being struck by lightening and not wishing to see what was going on, I dove to the floorboards face down. I then heard a static clinging sound, not more than a second after a loud clap of thunder vibrated the wooden floor boards that I lay on. I came to realize that the static clinging sound was a lightening bolt and it was close by, electricity slicing through the sky, Mother Nature style. Curiosity got the best of me and I raised my head up to take a peek off the starboard side. Another rigid jagged bolt of electricity slammed into the water only fifteen to twenty feet from the boat. I, out of a natural reaction, swung my head to the opposite direction, just in time to see a bolt cut through the water on the port side in about the same amount of distance from the boat. The clamoring from the thunder and the vibration throughout the boat was nothing like I ever heard or felt before. I cried out almost in tears, "we're gonna die." Gramp for a moment turned to me and let out a short burst of laughter, turned back, grabbed his shot bottle off the dashboard and took a swig. Now I knew after all these years living next door to him, he wasn't a drinking man, but he always kept a small shot bottle on board so that when he would reel in the "big one" he would celebrate with a drink. But I strongly felt now was not the time to be celebrating. Again I was crying out to him, pleading that he leave the liquor alone and please get us home. With another spout of laughter, but keeping a cool composure, he continued on. He always preferred a closed bow boat over an open bow, you sacrifice some space to fish from, but a closed bow won't as easily allow a rough sea to enter into the front of the boat, as an open bow would. The river roared and swelled, but guided by Gramp with both hands held loosely on the wheel to absorb shock, one eye on the compass and another peering through the rain pelted windshield, the closed "V" bow sliced and pounded a straight line towards home port.

After what seemed like endless time laying low on the floorboards, whether I became overwhelmed with a fear, or had fainted, the next thing I remembered was hearing "Here we are". As my eyes opened, the brightness of the partial sunshine lifted my spirits and as I looked through the windshield, our dock was only a hundred yards away. We were in Beadle Bay once again and a sensation of new life came over me, like being born again. I bellowed out "We're Alive!" Gramp said to me "here take a shot, I think you need it". With new life in me I thought sure, why not, but wow does that liquor burn going down. I looked over my left shoulder to see the dark blue shield of storm clouds steadily marching on to the east. The river and bay were calm now and with it came the assurance of a peaceful afternoon. Over and over again I thanked Gramp for bringing us back alive, but to him it was no big deal. As we neared the dock it was almost 12:30 PM, and Grandma stood there waiting. "That was quite a storm, Bernie you had me very worried. Don't you ever keep yourself and Scott out in a storm like that again. I almost called the Coast Guard." Gramp just kind of blew her off and suggested she could better spend her time in the kitchen. He loved the boat and water, that was his freedom and he wouldn't take kindly to anyone, not even his wife, telling him when to go and when to come. I jumped up on the dock, secured the ropes, gave Grandma a hug, ran off the dock to land and got down on all fours and kissed the ground.

Scott's experience with Bernie's expertise shows how Bernie made it through the difficult years. I think we all learned a lot of lessons from the Bootlegging Trio.